Jumbled

Jessica Batty

BookLeaf Publishing

India | USA | UK

Presentation by *BookLeaf Publishing*

Web: www.bookleafpub.com

E-mail: info@bookleafpub.com

ISBN:9789358318562

First edition 2023

DEDICATION

This book is for both Wilson Batty (Bill) and Edward Batty (Baby Eddie).

Two of the greatest men to have come and gone.

We miss you each and every day.

PREFACE

From me to you:

This collection of poetry varies in style and theme from page to page, just like life varies from day to day and year to year.

I hope for you to feel that you can find yourself somewhere within these pages. For you to feel that someone else understands that feeling which you're feeling or even that emotion that you've been avoiding. From elusive spiders to unrequited love and from the start of life through to grieving a death - You'll never walk alone.

Ice and Fire

I feel like ice and fire.
I feel the flames grow higher.
I feel the cold run deep in my veins.
I feel I have no desire.

I hear the reignited embers,
Once again catching light.
I sigh as my heart remembers,
Again, and again every night.

Full of hope for the future,
Yet hollow from the pain.
Toxic rage from experience,
Numb where my heart used to reign.

I look around and within me,
Desperate for something or someone to blame.
I fear that the fire will consume me,
And the ice feels like it burns all the same.

The flames are roaring on now,
Desperately to smother.
Whilst the ice spreads and hardens,
Each expands within the other.

Savage blues and manic orange,
battling for power.
Pushing and pulling, rising, and crashing,
They're ready to devour.

A whirling dangerous vortex grows now,
Building up within.
Impossible now to see one end,
And where the other begins.

Heaving and growing it swells to capacity,
Ready to spill over.
Burning and freezing all in its path,
How can it ever recover?

They say to trust the process,
My body is working through its pains.
But when the internal war is over,
How can my insides not be stained?

How will I not be changed forever,
By the molten turmoil within?
How can I say I feel better,
When I'm crumbling behind this grin?

I feel like ice and fire.
The polar opposites war and spin.
I feel that the two conspire,
To drag me down and down within.

But I know they cannot co-exist,
This tormented yin and yang.
But I must listen carefully,
For I'm the cage in which they sprang.

Oh...

Their body reacts instinctively:

Hairs stand on end...
Skin puckers with goosebumps...
Eyes widen, dilate, and squeeze shut...

Lips part with anticipation...
Breath ragged and audible...
Heart pounding and drumming, pumping wildly
in its cage.

The sensation spreads:

Chest heaving, rising, and falling...
Stomach in knots...
Sweat drips, tickles, and trickles down the
spine...

It's becoming unbearable:

Hands quiver reaching desperately...
Knees shaking below...
Toes beginning to curl...
Nerves fluttering around like a newly emerged
butterfly.

They look around and gasp…

Oh…   5

WHERE DID THE SPIDER GO?

Life: Loss: Grandad

Grandad is the wine brewer, the tea stewer, the
wood whittler, and the bird watcher.
Grandad is the drunken stripper, the biggest
joker, the cuddler, and the Metaxa drinker.
Grandad is the hug you didn't know you needed
and the songs you didn't know you knew.
Grandad is the pat on the knee whenever he sits
next to you.

Grandad is the voice from the kitchen, the
garden, and the wooden shed.
Grandad is telling you to rinse with warm water
before you go to bed.
Grandad is the best friend, the karaoke partner,
and the reason for your father.
Grandad is each and every Wilson of the family.
Grandad is singing "someday maybe my star
will smile on me".

Grandad is the melody to the song, without
which it seems wrong.
Grandad is the rhyme to this poem, but without
him.
It's going...
Going...

Gone.

Grief is yearning to hear "oh 'ello Love"
whenever you're alone.
Grief is the physical pain of seeing a Grandad
that's not your own.
Grief is wanting every notification to be an
accidental thumbs up on your part.
Grief is not knowing if you'll ever be able to
watch The Sound of Music again without falling
apart.

Grief is hearing "bye bye my Darling" and
knowing that this time he meant it.

Life without you seems so much darker in places
that before had light.
But what we lost down here, they gained up
there so now you help keep the night sky bright.

I'll hold my head up high and I wont be afraid of
the dark,
Because although gone with you are the eyes
full of spark,
I know I'll never walk alone.

A Muse-d

They say inspiration strikes.

That is, when it's not seemingly camouflaged itself into the darkest corners of your consciousness or the brightest whites of an empty page.

But IF inspiration strikes…

Who is it who does the striking?
A match does not strike itself.
So it must be stuck by us.

Me
You
Them
Us

People

It's no coincidence that ME is the bread to the sandwich that is MUSE.

So next time that illusive snake of a stimulus has you feeling abandoned…

Remind yourself - who did the striking?

If you can, be inspiring.

If you do, be inspired.

And if you can't…
Be your own damn inspiration.

Gone Too Soon

Here's to all the sweet, lovely things we never
got to do.
We spent months planning a lifetime of
memories we'd make with you.

We'd bundle up together rocking you softly on
the couch.
Then off we'd go for wintery walks with you
nestled like a Joey in the pouch.

We'd be excited for your first time on the baby
swing and to watch you fall asleep.
None of us knew these memories wouldn't be
ours to live and keep.

We spent hours hoping and praying, sleepless
eyes heaven bound under the moon.
But the angels came whilst you were sleeping
and then you were gone from us much too soon.

Didn't they know that we'd made plans with you
and had lots of people for you to meet?
Or didn't they much care that you'd not be here
in our arms for us to hold and keep?

We'd gaze at you star-fishing on your play-mat
your tiny hand in ours.
Then see the time in shock and realise we'd been
marvelling at your little self for hours.

We'd teach you how to ride a bike, hold tight
and say we won't let go.
Feel a million feelings bursting inside us as you
see your first fallen snow.

We'd planned to take you to the pumpkin patch,
brambles, and strawberry picking too.
Putting you on top of the fluffiest donkey and
laugh as we strolled along the beach next to you.

We'd dance around the kitchen whilst pots
bubble and boil away.
You'd stand atop our feet, holds hands steady as
we spin, sing and sway.

The list here could go on and on of the things
we'll never do.
Or the things we'd give and what we'd pay to be
there next to you.

But what we had with you down here will stay
with us forever.
We just hope you can feel our love for you up
there because it will never stop.

Never.

The Colour Green

Bearings found.
Blinds blink open.
Wheels screech.
Bags bundled.

Feet hit the ground.
Perfume sprayed.
Luggage found.
Trains: delayed.

The left-hand drive, the blue signs, the cats eyes
winking up at me on either side.
The drizzle, the windscreen blur, the radio…
The thing I've waited years for,
Finally coming in to view:
The colour green.

The rolling hills, the great expanse, the wheat
waving to me from the wind's hold.
The grass, the trees, the moss…
The thing I've waited years for,
Finally coming in to view:
The colour green.

The brook to stream, the river to sea, the sticks
peaking at me from below the bridge.
The salt, the sand, the shells…
The thing I've waited years for,
Finally coming in to view:
The colour green.

The cobbled streets, the wonky roofs, the
puddles reflecting the day's grey canopy back to
me.
The thing I've waited years for,
Finally coming in to view:
The colour green.

I see it.
I smell it.
I feel it.

That earthy, heavy scent that accompanies each
and every one of my childhood memories.
That comforting cosy embrace of nature.
Not manicured, or fake,
Not carefully created for the camera's sake.
The thing I've waited years for,
Finally coming in to view:
The calmest colour to be seen,
The proof that nature reigns supreme,
The vibrant hues of each leaf's gleam,
Finally, the colour green.

Sunrise Sunset

How to choose between dusk and dawn?
Each one making me feel cosy.
A warm cocoon of nature's glow.
At peace with the world around me.

The soft pink-orange fades to blues,
And the clouds hang there like wardens.
A canvas covered in my favourite hues,
As the world resets its rhythm.

Morning dew drops sparkling softly,
As they sit atop the spiders' webs.
Evening mist slowly swirling in,
Eerily crawling as it flows and ebbs.

The owls of every colour eyes,
Ready to pounce upon their prey,
Green, yellow and orange open in surprise,
Hunting through the dark until the dawning of
the day.

The moon glows ghostly in the sky,
Hanging solicitously above us each night.
I search there for the face I've seen before,
Dusk 'til dawn nature's comforting nightlight.

The waxing, waning or colossal full view of
Luna,
Gives way to the rising of the sun.
I itch and fizz and with both peace and
excitement,
As a new day has ended or just begun.

Insert

Sometimes I feel so ________________ .
I look forward to ________________ but feel so

________________ .

Sometimes I just feel ________________ .
I yawn and start my day with a ________________

.

I finish up with a huge ________________ .

Sometimes I can feel ________________ .
I say ________________ but I really mean

________________ .

Sometimes I want to feel ________________ .
I try ________________ but I wind up

________________ .
I've had ________________ and I've also had

________________ .

Sometimes I don't feel ________________ .
I should ________________ but instead I'll

________________ .

Sometimes I've felt ________________ .

I know _______________ so I can

_______________ .

I've heard _______________ but then I feel

_______________ .

I've never felt _______________ .
I've always wanted to feel _______________ .

I try to make others feel _______________ .
If I can feel _______________ I know I can

_______________ .

One day I'll feel so _______________ .

Winter

Winter is…
Cosy season.

Time spent with family, friends or even a cuddle
with the cat.

The trees outside frozen, bony, and bare.
The ones we put up inside are decorated without
an inch to spare.

Images of white quilted fields dotted with
clusters of sheep,
Come into our minds as we drift off to sleep.

Eyes peak open in the morning praying for
snow.
The excitement of this something some of us
will never outgrow.

Our breath comes out hot from our swathed
shivering selves.
Then turns ice-cold into mist as it floats, tumbles
and swells.

The joy of searching for our favourite woollen
gloves, scarf, and hat.
Leaving warm defrosted prints where we've
walked, touched, and sat.

Shops, bars, and cafes filled with lights glowing
amber, welcoming, and warm.
Full of couples, friends, and families, the crowds
flurry and swarm.

Pavements sparkle and glisten like frozen
kaleidoscopes.
Each of us with our own traditions for the season
filled with pious hopes.

Autumn

Autumn is…
Hibernation season.

Time spent baking or crafting or even curled up
with a good book.

The trees outside shedding their red and fiery
hues.
The ones we love to crunch and kick up with our
shoes.

Images of snuffling hedgehogs collecting
materials for their snug toasty nest.
And squirrels stashing chestnuts ready for next
Spring's annual hunting quest.

Peeking into the oven to see the pie and cookies
long awaited.
The excitement and pride of seeing something
your own two hands created.

Our cheeks rosy pink as the icy winds bite and
scold.
They flush in colour as temperatures battle
between cosy warm and cold.

The joy of glittering fireworks which burst
across the night sky.
Leaving multifaceted rainbows and smoke as the
embers slowly die.

Apple bobbing, pumpkin carving and running
through corn mazes.
Each of us clinging to snacks and one another as
the bonfire dances and blazes.

Sleepy late sunrises, nights draw in and we draw
the curtains early.
Fog lays heavy and low on an evening as it
snakes along ghostly and pearly.

Nightly Terror

I wake and I can feel it.
I feel it prickling up my skin,
And down deep within.
Churning in the pit of my stomach,
The feeling that you're not alone.

It pushes and presses,
There in the darkness,
That lays heavy upon me.
The feeling you're being watched by the
unknown.

I hear my heart and brain racing.
My pulse banging wildly in my ears.
I feel my face flush and my body shiver.
The feeling that there's nothing you can do.

It takes the air from my lungs,
As though I can only exhale,
No intake to catch my breath.
The feeling you want to run but the darkness
stops you.

I struggle against my own body.
My mind in flight but my limbs cannot fight.

I feel my hair and sheets slick and stick to my
skin.
The feeling of wishing you could reach for the
light.

It has me pinned here against my will,
The dense darkness which fills the room,
As it presses my limbs into the bed below.
The feeling of screaming but no sound passes
your lips.

The feeling of waiting for it to be over.
The nightly terror.

Explorer Tourer

The first time visiting a place is like no other.
Walking through streets and seeing it all with
fresh eyes.

The curve of the path, the arch of the windows,
The way the black striped buildings lean over
you as you walk.
Standing stately above the chaos, if only these
walls could talk.

The first time visiting a place is exploring the
unknown.
Walking around each bend and not knowing
what you'll find.

The native dialect or entirely different
languages,
The sweet scent of sugary goods floating down
from the town's best bakery.
Streams of hungry mouths in zig zag lines as
they stand outside patiently.

The first time visiting a place is the adrenaline
you feel.

Not minding at all at having to search the entire
place for the one thing you need.

The museums, the galleries, the historic railway
stations.
The punny street names still fresh enough to be
appreciated.
Posing excitedly for a photo to make that one
person laugh as much as you.

The first time visiting is like seeing it all in high
definition.
The blues somehow bluer, the greens seem
greener, even the brickwork looks brighter.

The slope of the beach, the wave of the trees.
You daydream yourself a life: here's where
you'd get that morning smoothie, there's your
new local.
Why have you never considered living on stilts
before?

Zig Zag

The walking contradiction.
Life as societal targets:

Zig-
Always be patient.
Zag -
But don't wait around too long.

Zig-
Be your own person.
Zag-
Let him make you his fantasy.

Zig-
Speak your mind and speak plain so as not to
confuse or lead them on.
Zag -
Don't be honest about how they have made you
feel in case you make them feel bad.

Zig -
Always make an effort to appear young and
youthful.
Zag -

Don't be jailbait it's unfair, how can they control themselves.

Zig -
Conceal the tiredness, the hurt and the broken dreams.
Zag -
Don't wear too much makeup, it makes you look high maintenance.

Zig -
Dress for the occasion, the job, the man.
Zag -
Don't look like you have aspirations, it's desperate and unattractive.

Zig -
Don't rely on him to provide, it's 2023.
Zag -
Don't earn more than him, think how that makes him feel.

Zig -
Be the best mother you can be, always be there for your children.
Zag -
You don't work? I thought you wanted equality?

Zig -

Natural beauty is always best, don't be fake.

Zag -

Why don't you look like these pictures online?

Zig-

Don't worry, all attention is good attention.

Zag –

Behaving like that, you were asking for it.

Zig -

Don't be a prude, let them see and be proud of your femininity.

Zag -

Dressed like that she had it coming.

Zig –

Always be polite, kind and smile.

Zag-

He was kind, now you owe him something.

Zig-

Be a strong independent woman and go by yourself.

Zag-

Getting a taxi alone, she should have known.

Dear Mini Me

Dear Mini Me

I wish that I could tell you,
All of the amazing things you'll do.
Despite the trials and tribulations,
You're no doubt going through.

It's going to be truly amazing to see,
The places you'll go and the people you'll know,
Remember not to let them or that stop you,
They can't dull or tarnish your glow.

Please be mindful who you spend your time on,
Time is the most precious thing you will ever
have.
Time to love and time to learn,
Time to streak your face with tears as you cry
and laugh.

There will be so many stages of your life,
Where you think 'That's it. I'm done.'
Done growing, done changing, done trying,
I've had enough, I can't go on'.

You'll feel what you give isn't good enough,

But that simply isn't true.
Your thoughts and kindness, your energy,
Noone can be a better you.

Eighteen is not your destiny,
And neither is thirty-two.
You're never done developing,
And growing into a deeper better you.

Everyone will give you their opinion,
They'll dress it up as fact,
Most only trying to help you,
But all lying in wait, for how you'll react.

But what do you hear in a dark room,
When it's only you and your truest thoughts?
You'll find the answer of what to do there,
Not by internalising every other person's 'do's
and 'do not's.

It's hard to truly love yourself,
We all struggle at times with this.
But work to be your own biggest cheerleader,
Don't get sucked into self-doubt's dark abyss.

Prioritise treating yourself kindly,
I know you're trying your best.
You've got one body, one mind in this life,

Treat them both well, allowing them equal time
to rest.

I love you now and forever,
The past and future version of current me.
Remind yourself of that with this letter,
My dearest Mini Me.

X

Spring

Spring is…
Fresh starts season.

Time spent making plans, comparing calendars,
and learning new skills.

The trees outside are born again, life ready to
renew.
The tiny buds and bulbs ready to burst as
delicate petals try break through.

Images of fields of tulips, cotton tailed bunnies,
and chicks hatching from their shells.
Freshly cut grass, blossoming meadows,
chocolate eggs adding to the myriad of soothing
smells.

Eyes taking in the explosion of colour which
shoots up from the ground.
Fields, farms, and woodland displaying the
beautiful patchwork nature has created all
around.

Our layer upon layer of woolly winter warmers
ready to be shed.

We peel them off week by week eagerly
anticipating the warmth of months ahead.

The joy of baby animals innocently blinking up
glassy eyed to stare at you.
Leaving life-long perfect memories of that
special moment between just you two.

Prismatic colours thrown across the clouds in
rainbows as the everchanging weathers clash.
Children, adults and even dogs pulling on their
wellies ready to jump and splash.

Raindrops run and streak down windowpanes
with their gentle pitter-patter.
April showers and thunderstorms, the perfect
blend of chaos and calm from the latter.

Summer

Summer is…
Holiday season.

Time spent building sandcastles, eating alfresco,
and running from the wasps.

The trees outside are full of life, sun-ripened
fruit ready for the drop.
The branches full and bristling, birds' nests
balanced precariously, fighting on top.

Images of winding vineyards, busy coastlines,
festivals full.
Frantically packing outdoor events into just
three months, leaving not a moment spare or
dull.

Searching up and down each row for the last
space in the carpark.
Setting up your carefully packed picnic in the
outdoor cinema as it gets dark.

Our skin tingles with the sudden shock of being
exposed to the warm breezy air.

After months of sheltering from rain, snow and
wind, our arms adjust exposed and bare.

The joy of spotting a sleepy grey seal or a red
deer stalking nearby at night.
Clock changes giving way to longer sun-filled
days and nights still filled with light.

The sun rises to greet you in the morning, cloud
spotting and the twinkling of shooting stars.
BBQs, garden parties, floppy hats, crowded
tables, and benches outside bars.

Beaches, rivers, lakes, and woods beckon and
dare us to explore.
Forbidden trails off the beaten track to discover
and make memories galore.

Leaf in the Wind

I saw a leaf blowing in the wind.

Holding on for dear life.

I saw how its colours were being drained,

Greens fading to yellow and brown.

I saw the once smooth edges curl,

How they thinned, crisp and jagged now.

I saw a leaf blowing in the wind.

Clinging desperately to the tree's bark.

I saw how it flitted around,

Tossed side to side by the unforgiving winds.

I saw how the once strong stem would bend,

Mocking fluidity to save its own life.

I saw a leaf blowing in the wind.

Despite feeling the world against it.

I saw where the leaf had come from.

I felt hope it had once felt.

I saw the leaf there before me.

I heard of it's determination.

I saw the leaf.

I felt for the leaf.

I am the leaf in the wind.

Evolution of the Writing on
the Wall

When I first met your mum, I was greeted with
flowers,
To then be critiqued over the next days and
hours.
It started with questions, interest and a gift,
But given enough time I felt the energy shift.
I told you of this, hoping that I could make you
see,
But reflected in that relationship was a mirror of
you and me.

Wear this.
Push this.
Lift this.
Show this.

I've heard it before that 'eyes are the window to
the soul'.
But you covered yours for months, another form
of control.
I wanted to know you and thought and hoped
that I did.
But from the very beginning, parts of you had
been intentionally hid.

Try this.
Listen to this.
Taste this.
Drink this.

It started off small so that I didn't see it coming,
The warped twisted world our relationship was
becoming.
The multiple accounts, the comment here and
there.
I thought that you loved me, hoped you did, so
told myself I didn't care.

Shave this.
Lose this.
Have this.
Trust this.

I embraced all aspects of your culture, the
music, and the clothes.
You were adamant that one day you were going
to propose.
Meeting with my family and asking for their
blessing,
I just didn't see the anger and hatred you'd been
suppressing.

Say this.
Feel this.

Think this.
Do this.

From car crashes to fights and camping by the
lakes,
I'm kicking myself now for not seeing all of my
mistakes.
The photo edits, the paranoia, the forcing
yourself on top,
I wish that I'd seen it sooner, stood up faster, and
brought it to a stop.

Work this.
Own this.
Believe this.
Follow this.

We said that moving countries would be the
biggest of our tests,
But feeling like a Green Card was far too much
to digest.
I came here alone, always with the plan for you
to follow,
But 'if you loved me, you'd marry me' was too
big a pill for me to swallow.

Be this.
Like this.
Accept this.

Live like this.

Different continents and time zones really gave
me enough space to think.
Our love had been damaged beyond repair,
chink after fatal chink.
The drunken shouts, the sober comments, and
the way you'd never listen.
The things I'd do would never be enough, even
after bailing you out of prison.

I don't like this.
I don't want this.
I don't deserve this.
I won't be forced into this.

I told you no and suffered the consequences, as
your behaviour began to spiral.
But given the threats, the harassment and
stalking, it felt key to my survival.
So now there's over 4,000 miles of space and the
Indian Ocean between us two.
It seems a lot but still feels less of a gap than
sharing a bed with you.

It's Not Me - It's You

I know you'll think this is about you.
Who else could it possibly be?
Who else could have meant something?
Who else could have done that to me?

You'll think it's you when I say I fell hard,
I fell quick, and ultimately got hurt.
But you'll only tell everyone it's about you,
When I say something to insinuate you were
always sweeter than dessert.

You'll know it's you when I say I felt cheated,
In the way you led me on.
But you'll only tell everyone it's about you,
When I say you were the only person I could
rely upon.

You'll think it's you when I say wasted my time,
Sleep and energy, waiting up for drunken
late-night calls.
But you'll only tell everyone it's about you,
When I admit I opened up, tried not to throw up
my emotional brick walls.

You'll know it's secretly about you,

When I say we discussed our childhoods and
compared the Man in the Moon.
But you'll only tell everyone it's about you,
When it comes to making you look good, as if I
couldn't help but swoon.

You'll know it's always about you,
When I say that you betrayed my patience, trust,
and heart.
But you'll only admit that it was all about you,
When it's implied that without you my world
falls apart.

You'll know damn well it's about you,
When I say I was clearly just a confidence or
ego boost.
But you'll never admit it to yourself,
That you've not been the same since the summer
that we were introduced.

So, I guess I'll never admit that it's about you,
I can't bring myself to say it to your face.
But I know deep down you already know,
That all along I loved you, then found out you
were only in it for the chase.

Ode to Teachers

45

The life of a Teacher used to be seen as one that
was sweet,
One with job satisfaction when they left work,
complete.

Seen to take your little acorns and build them
into great trees.
The person you'd trust with their welfare and to
clean their scraped knees.

Well, they now feel exhausted burnt out to their
very cores.
They went into it for the children but spend
more time comparing them and their scores.

How can we expect these people to continue to
give up more?
When already they carry home hundreds of
books and burdens, work never done and left at
the door.

They're there when your child needs a friend, a
Tutor, a Nurse or just a calming hug.

They greet every child and gift with joy,
throughout another season where they contract
every bug.

They beam at all your child learns to do,
bursting with surprise and pride.
They'll always do it for the children, despite
feeling emotionally they're dying inside.

So, here's not to the 'outstanding' teachers,
But to the (somehow) STILL standing teachers.

Though they deserve more than the full bottle,
For everything they've done and gone through
full throttle,
Let's show appreciation, cheers and raise a glass,
To those who'd do it all again, out of love for
our children of their class.

Life Lessons From Fairy Tales:

Good will always prevail, they just need to go through hell first.
Innocence will always win, they just have to be distrusted first.

Don't take the short cut in life, you'll end up getting there later.
Don't judge a book by it's cover, wait until you read the first chapter.

A cottage in the woods is a dice roll, it could really go either way.
A castle is also a flip of a coin, it really depends on the owner.

Never eat the food made by a stranger.
Never eat strange buildings made from food.

If you see a thin sharp object, resist the urge to poke it.
If you see a long rope of hair hanging from a tower, rescue it.

Don't build your house out of sticks, straw, or anything flammable.
Always be kind to your stepmother or move out completely.

Talking to animals in the forest is normal, at least the cute ones anyway.
Animals stopping you to chat in the forest? Quickly, run away!

Oh, and don't forget…
Never wear slip on shoes!

www.ingramcontent.com/pod-product-compliance
Lightning Source LLC
LaVergne TN
LVHW021252200726
843509LV00012B/1652